I0485145

Charcoal & Conté

by MILA FOX

Charcoal & Conté

by MILA FOX

Illustrated by Mila Fox

COPYRIGHT © 2019 by Mila Fox

ALL RIGHTS RESERVED.

10 9 8 7 6 5 4 3 2

Meant 2 Bea Publications
Providence, Rhode Island

4

MORE BY THIS AUTHOR

Bare to the Bones: Charcoal Figure Art
Beautiful, Be-YOU-tiful, YOU
Be-YOU-tiful Crusade: Lend a Hand
Be-YOU-tiful Crusade: Don't be Afraid
Be-YOU-tiful Crusade: Bullying Can
Happen At Any Age
Be-YOU-tiful Crusade: Sibling's Day
CHIC-ipedia
Fifty-Eight

Line

Environment

Bone Structure

Self-Portrait

Line

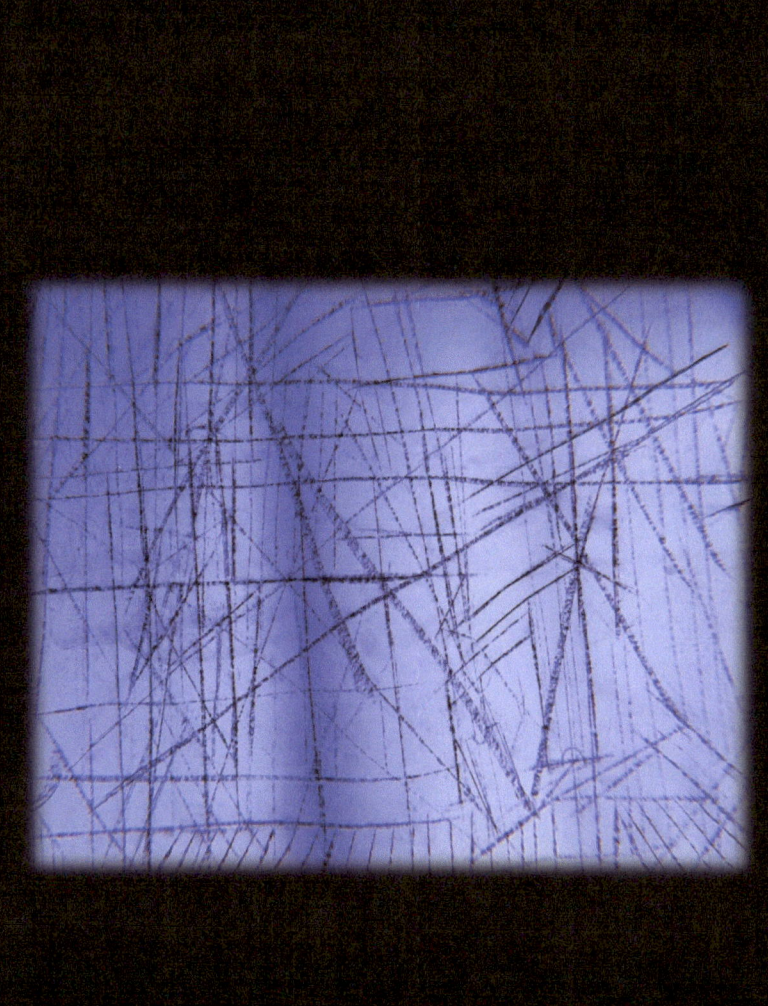

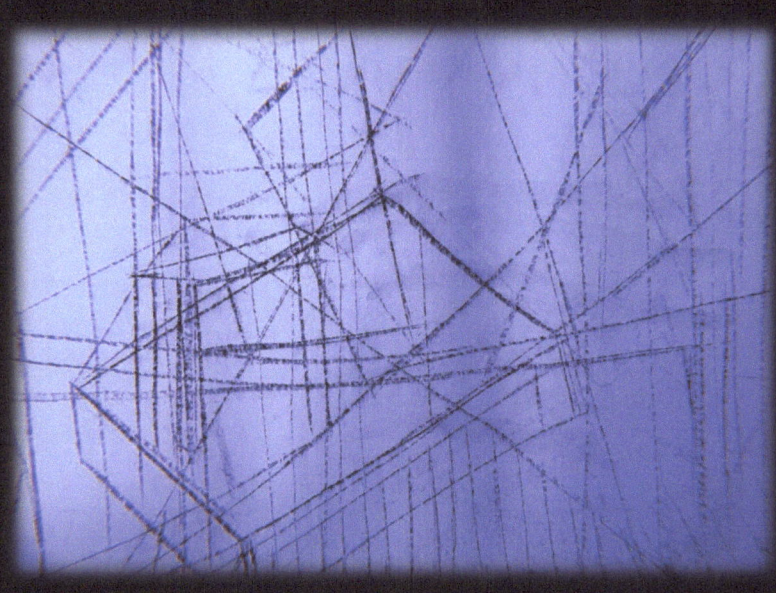

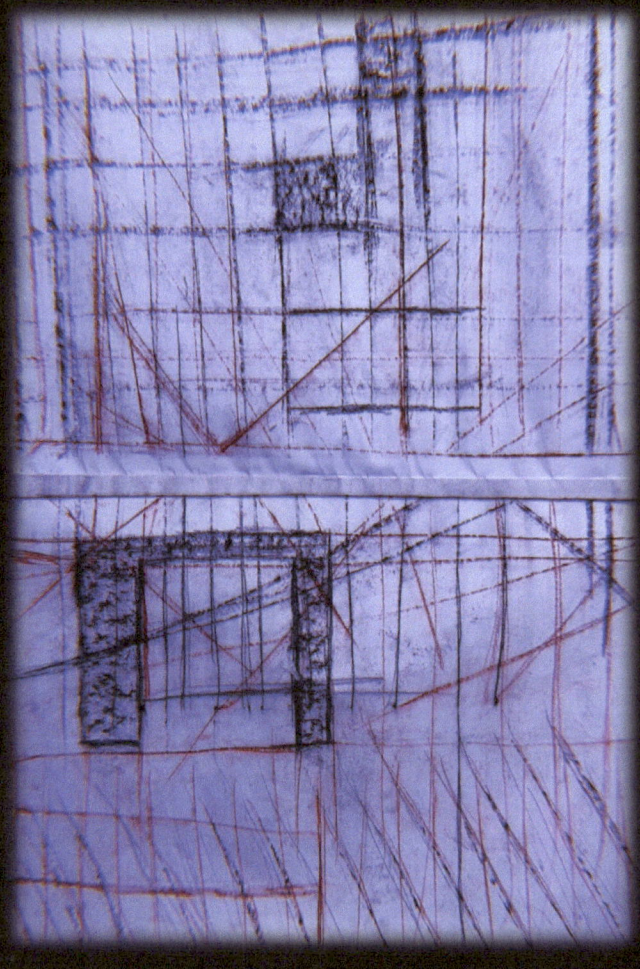

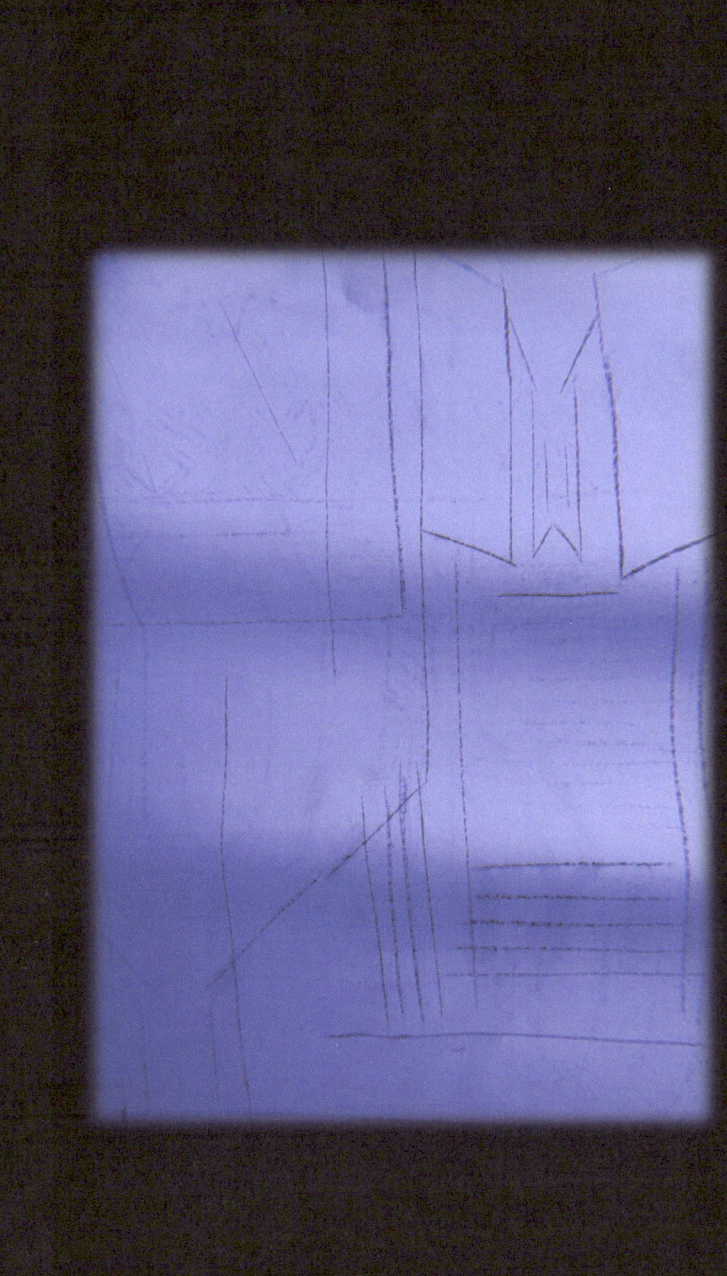

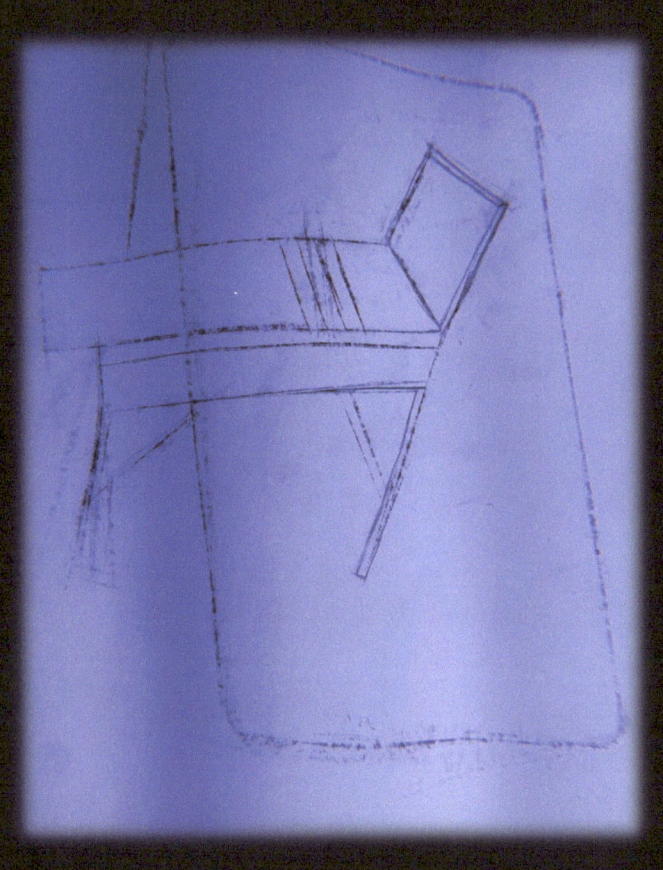

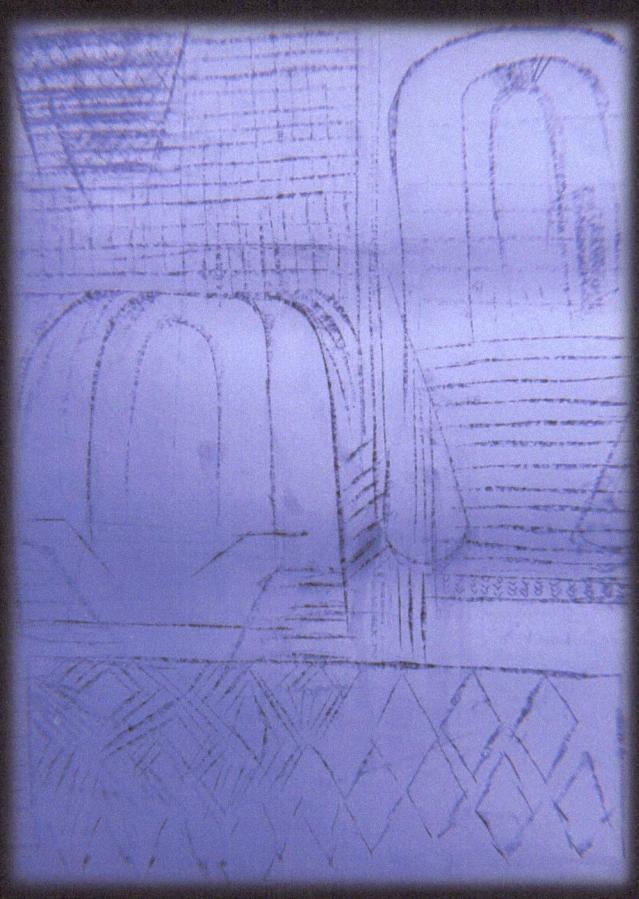

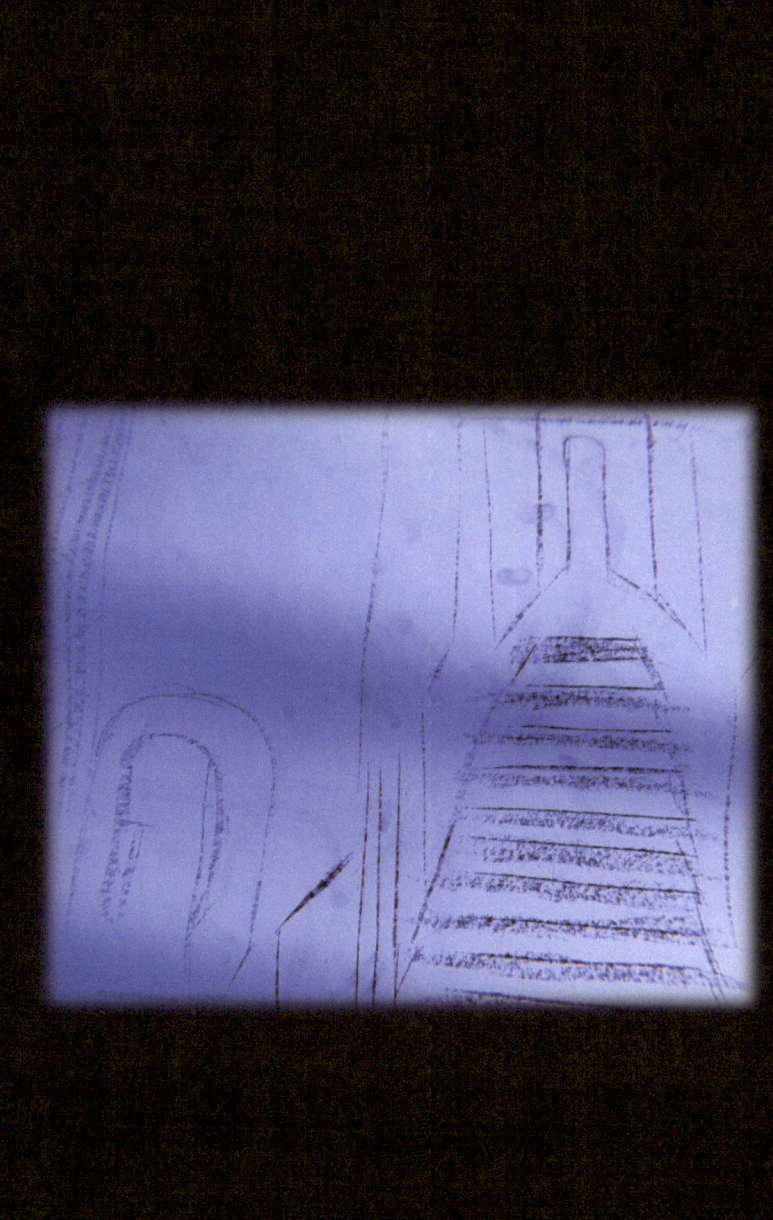

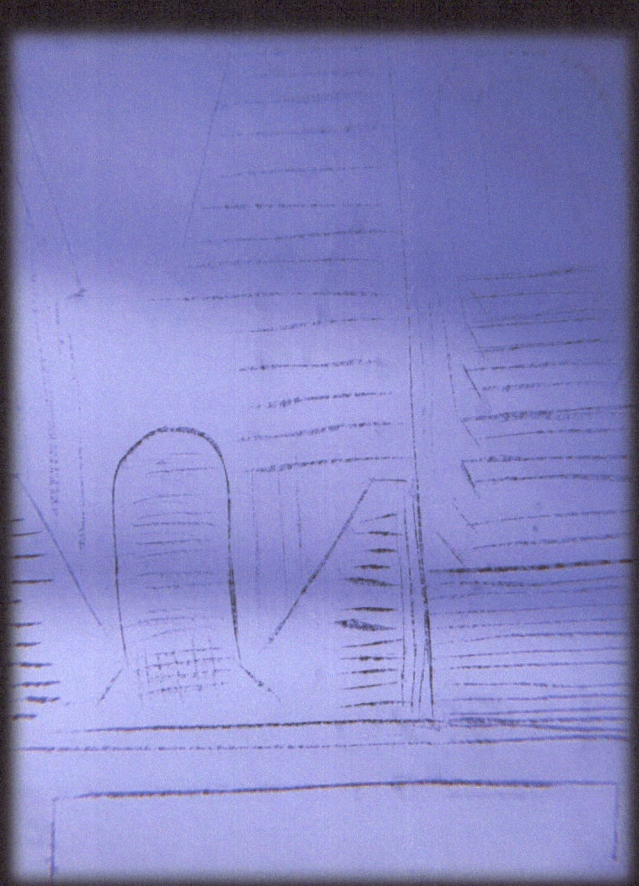

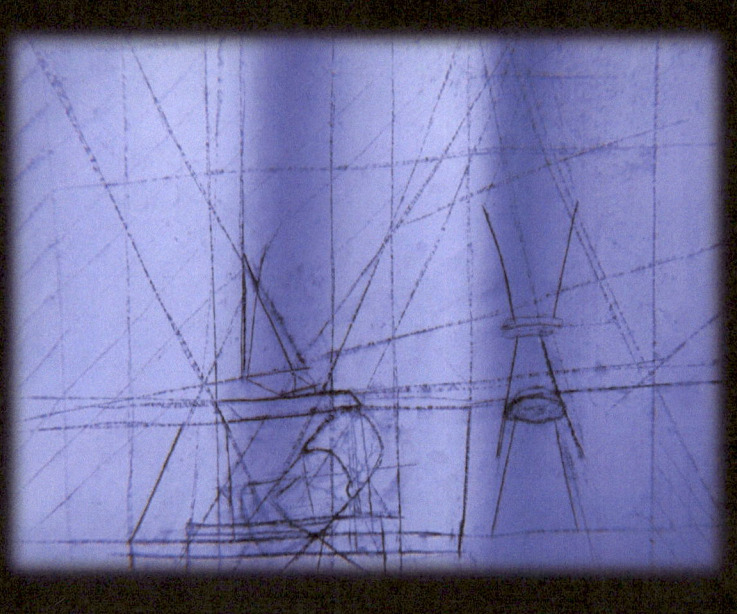

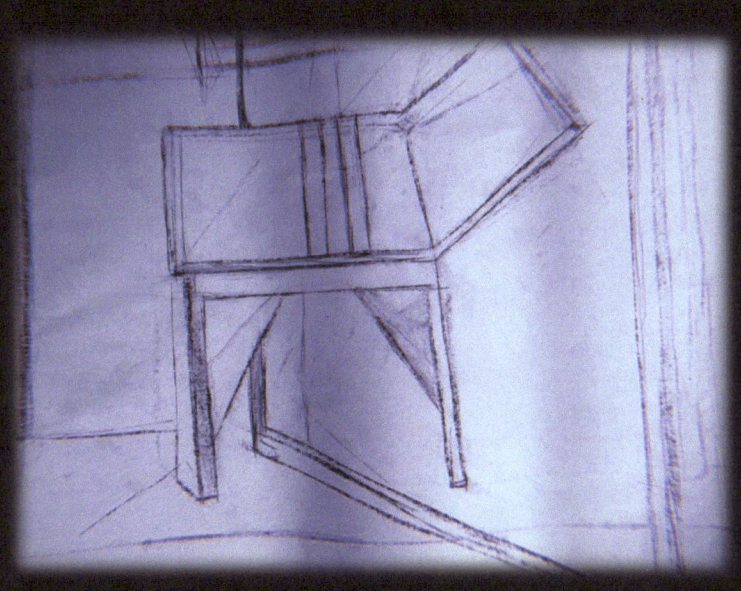

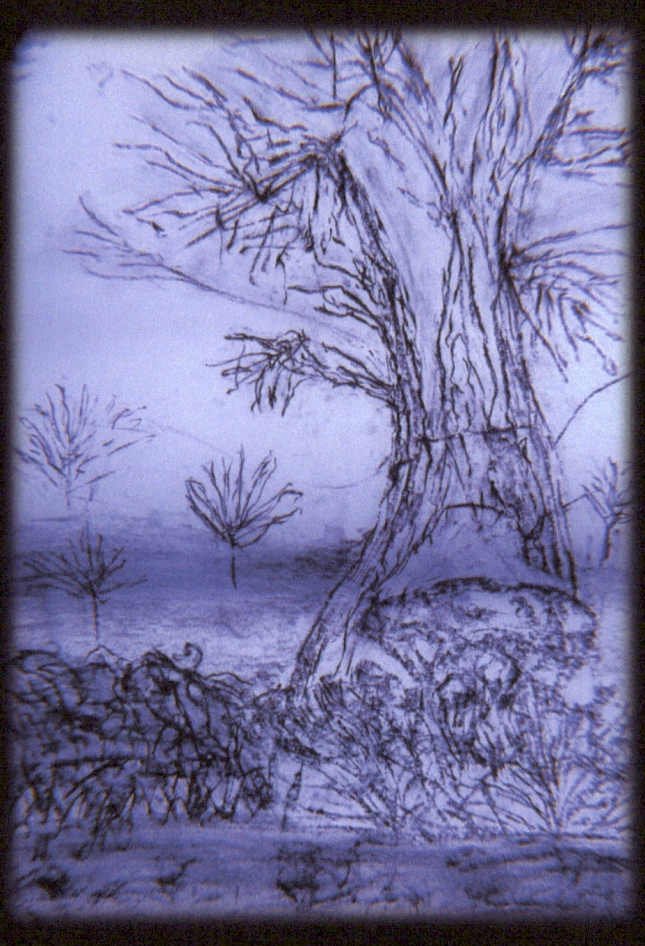

Environment

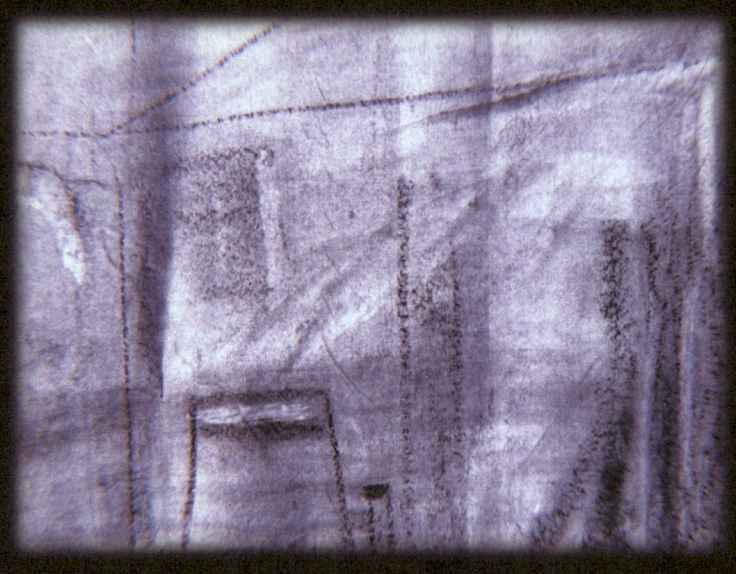

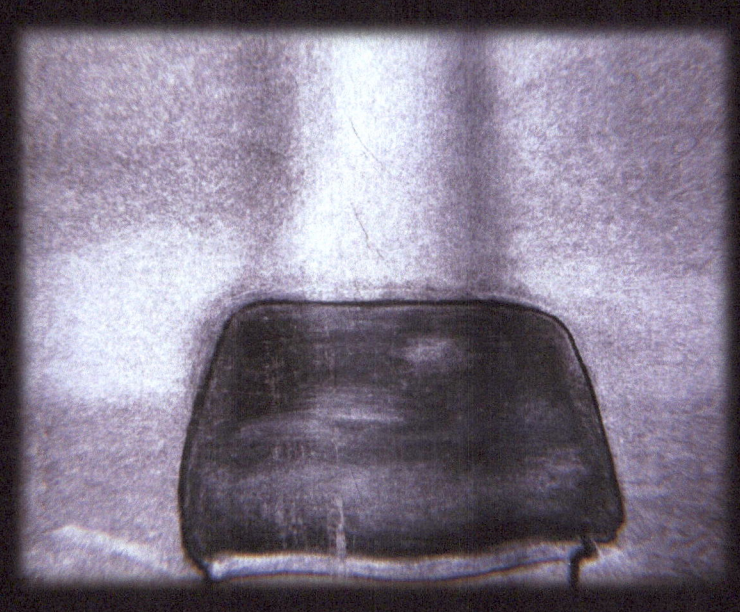

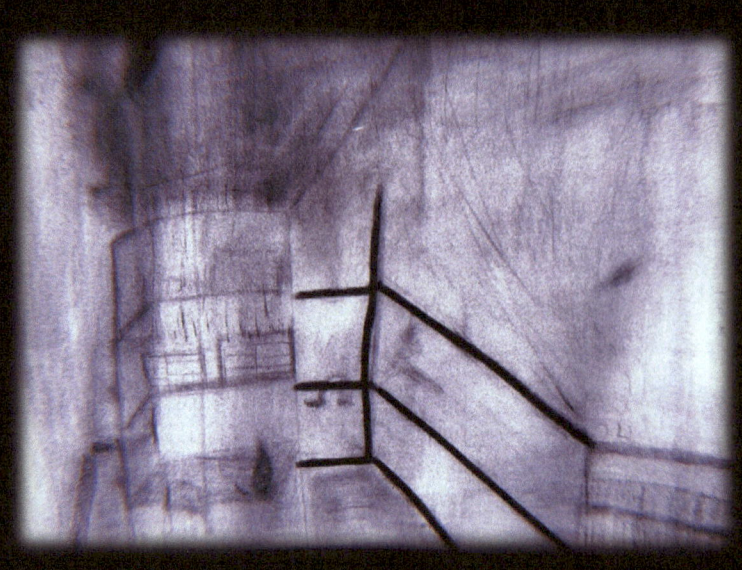

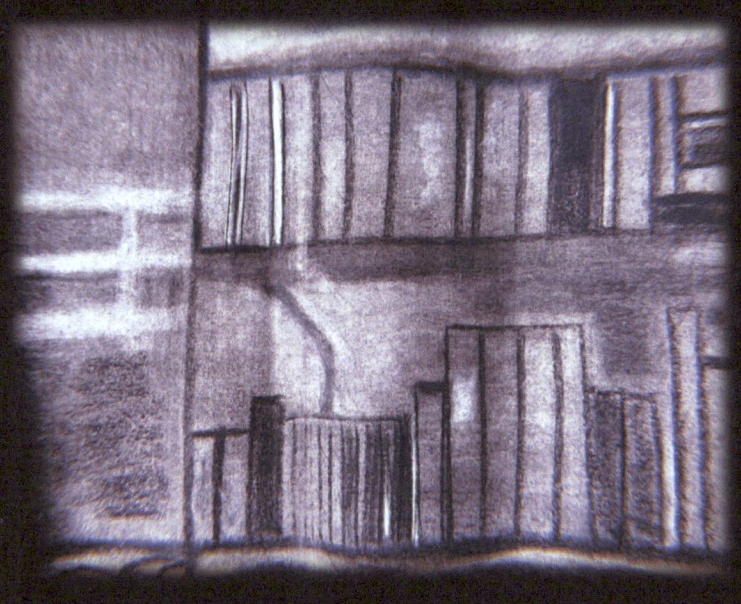

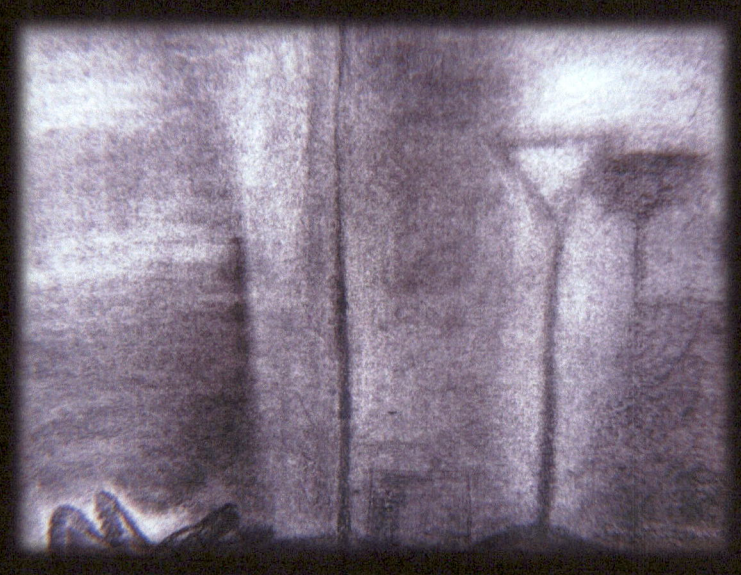

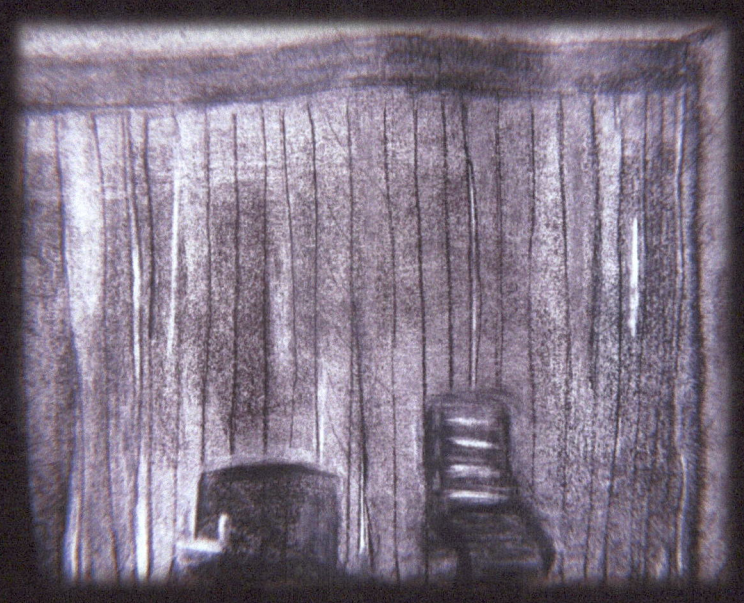

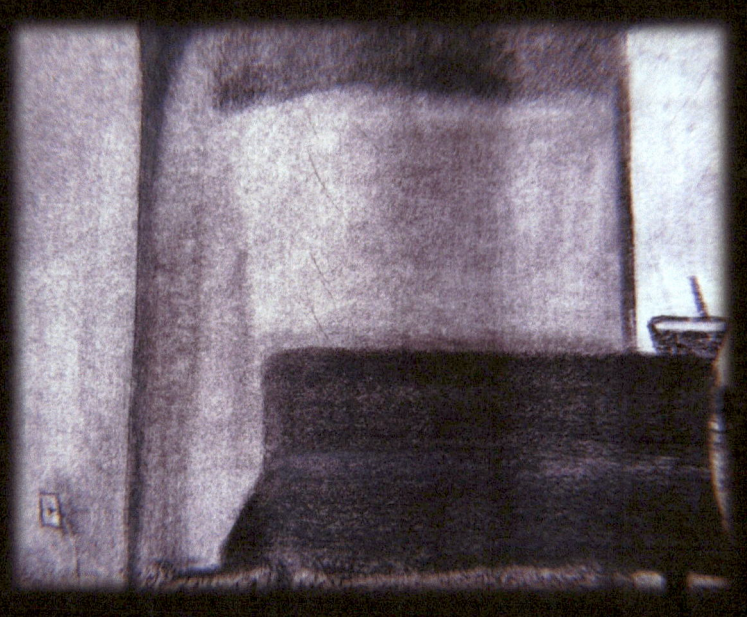

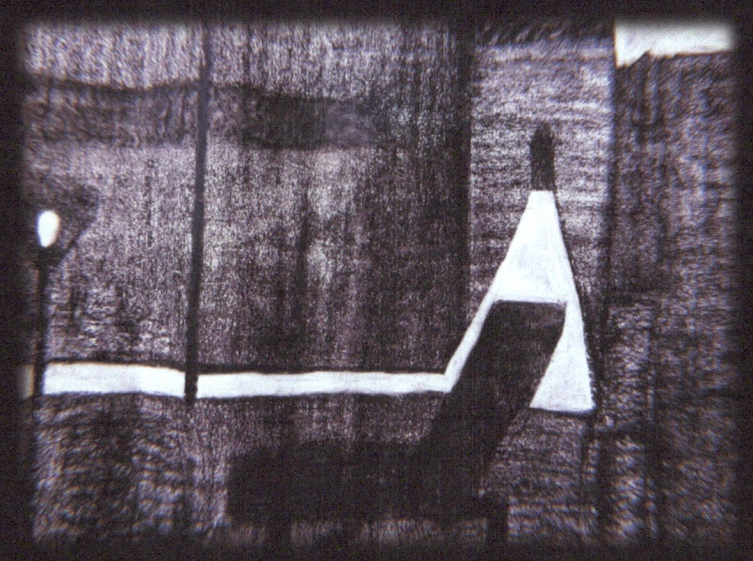

Bone Structure

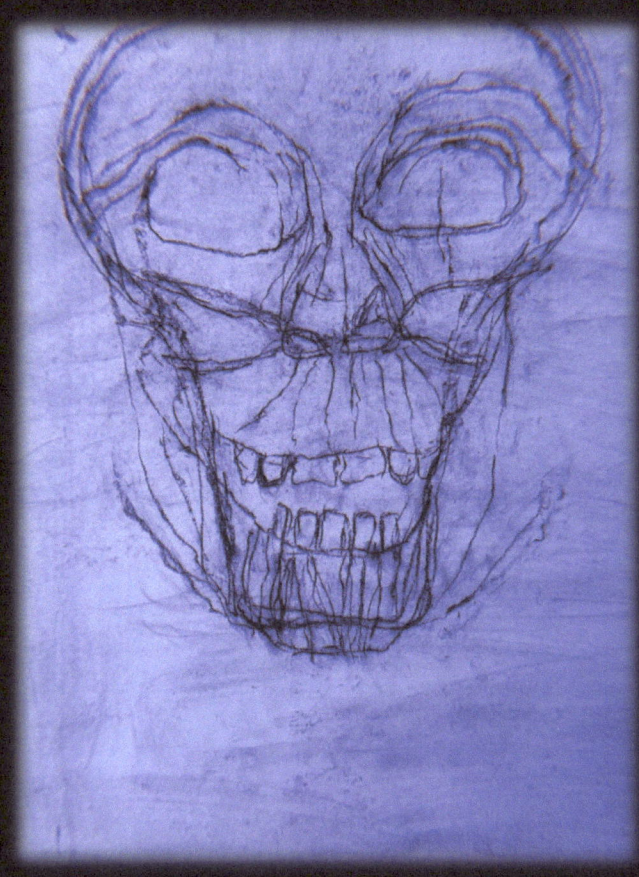

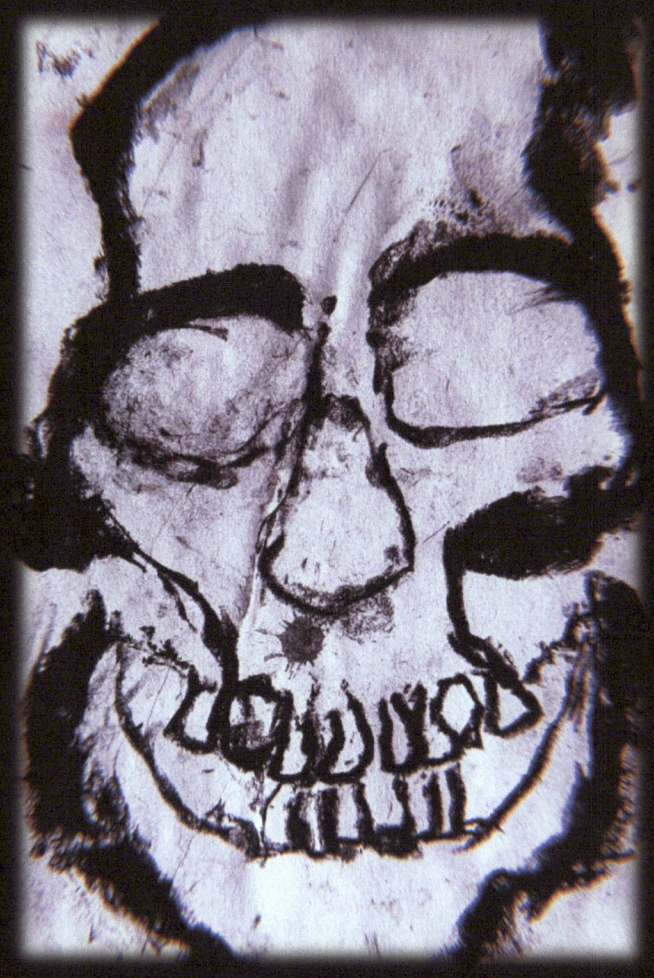

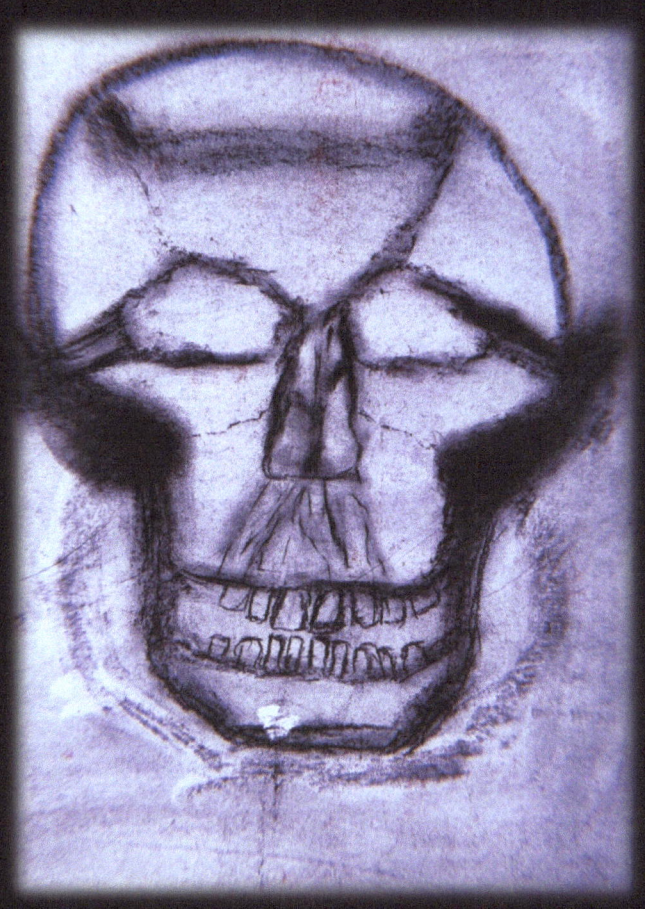

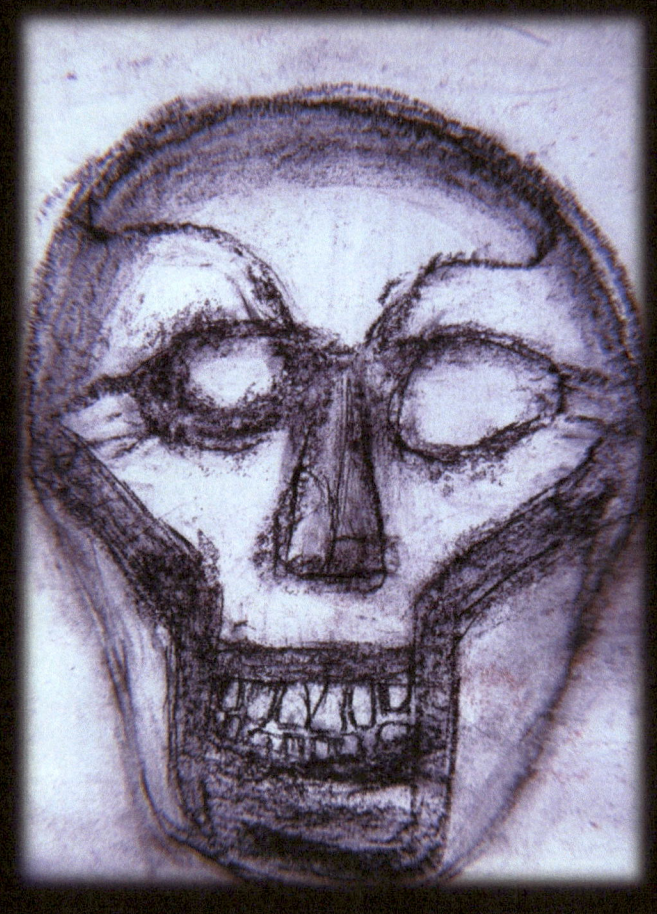

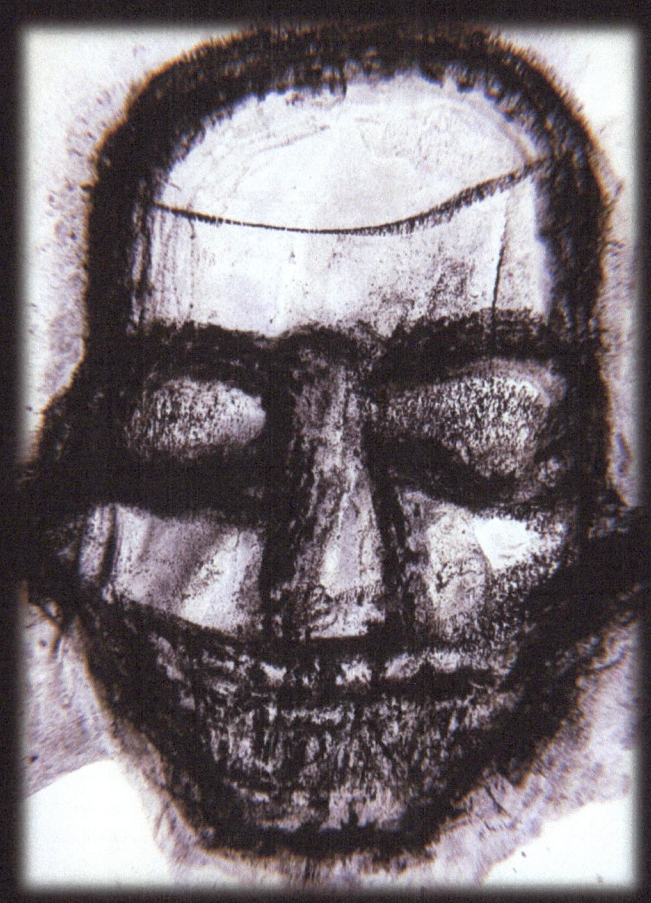

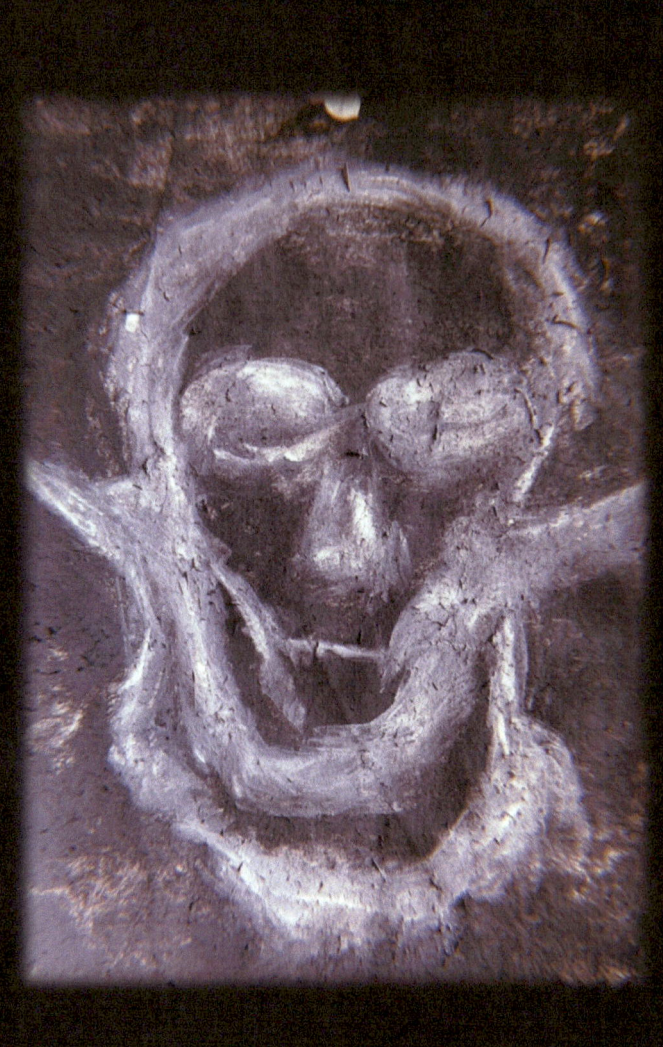

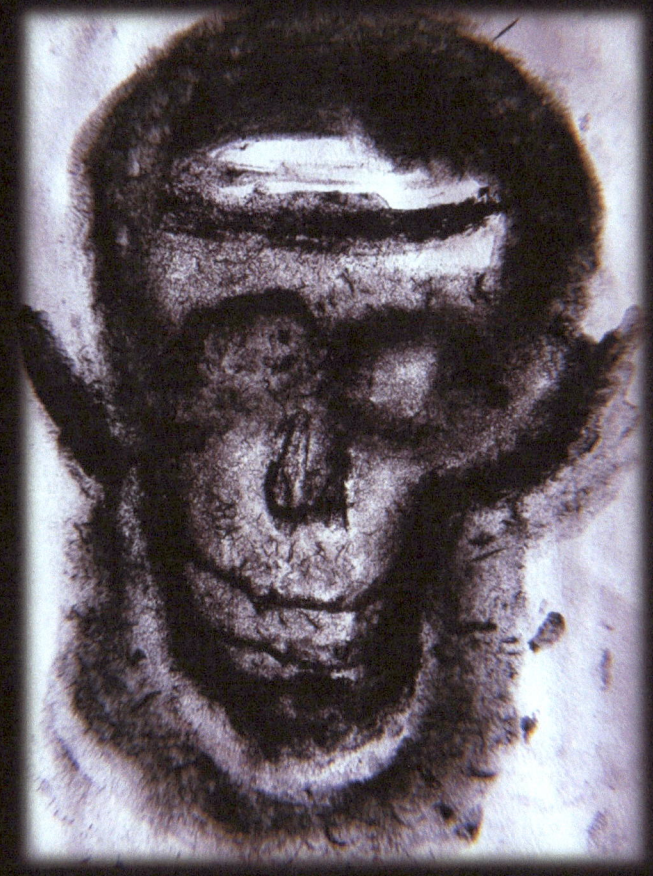

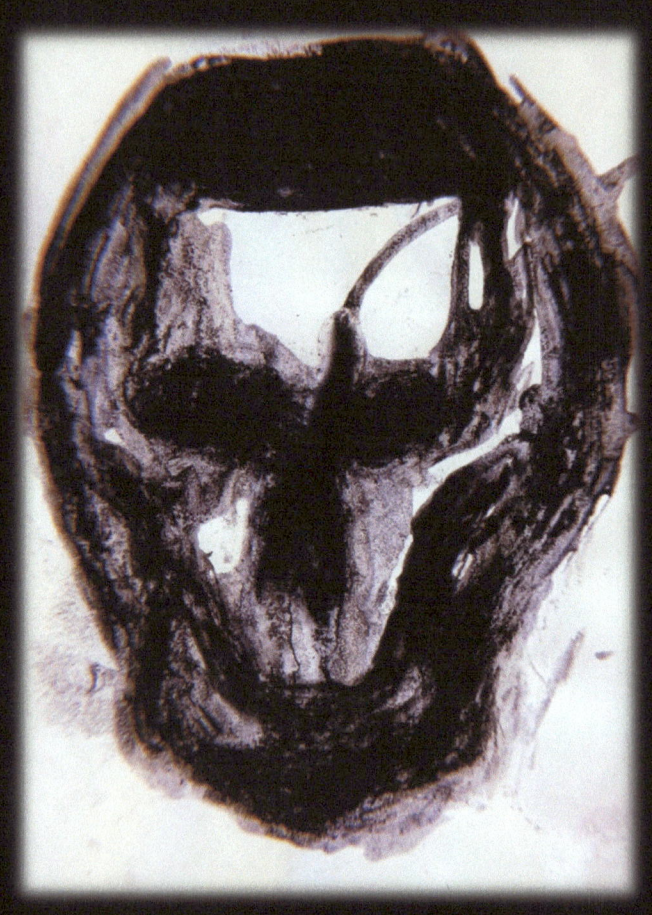

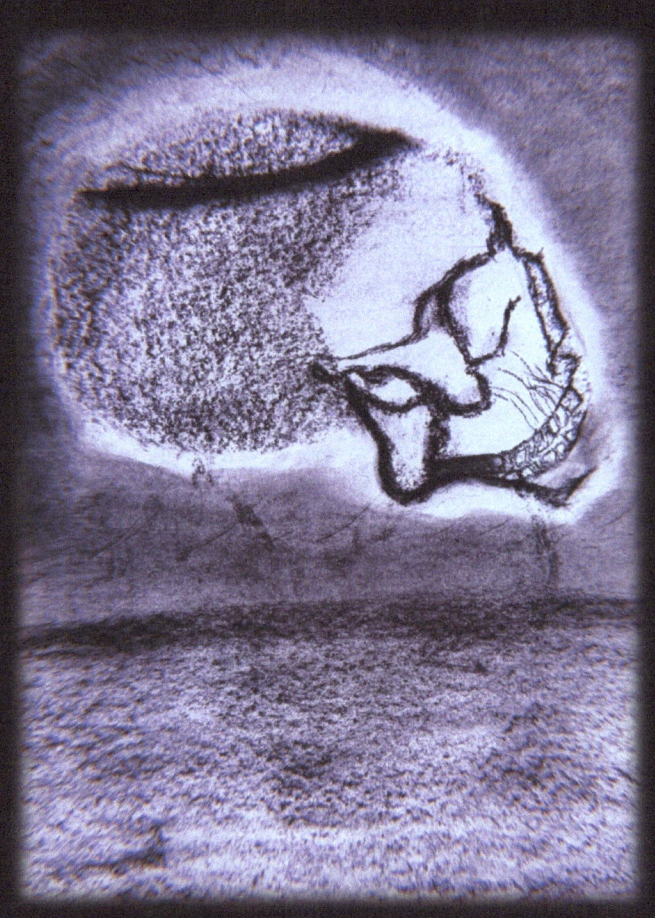

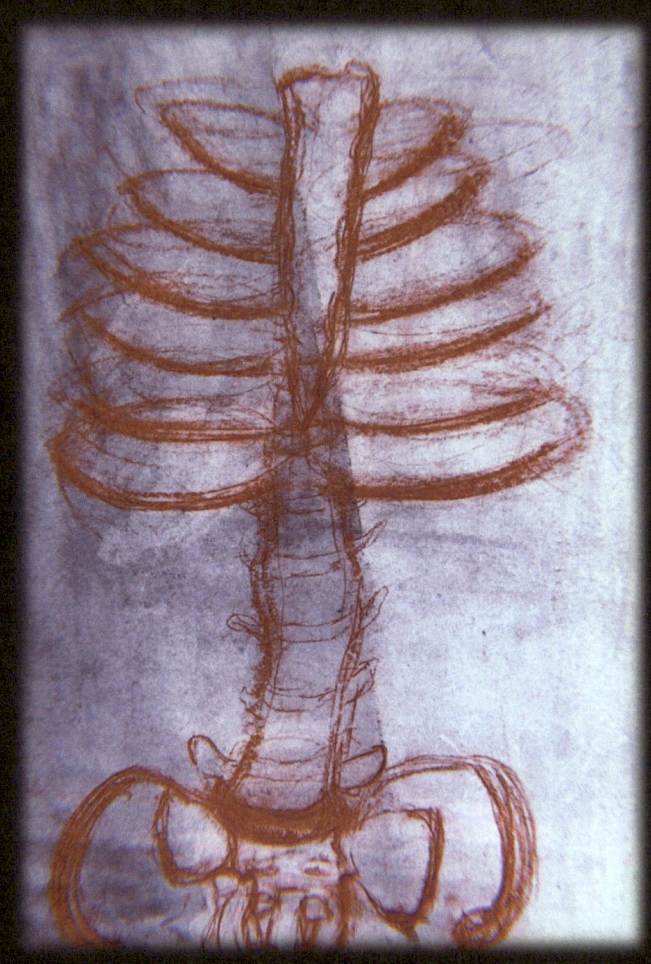

Self-Portrait

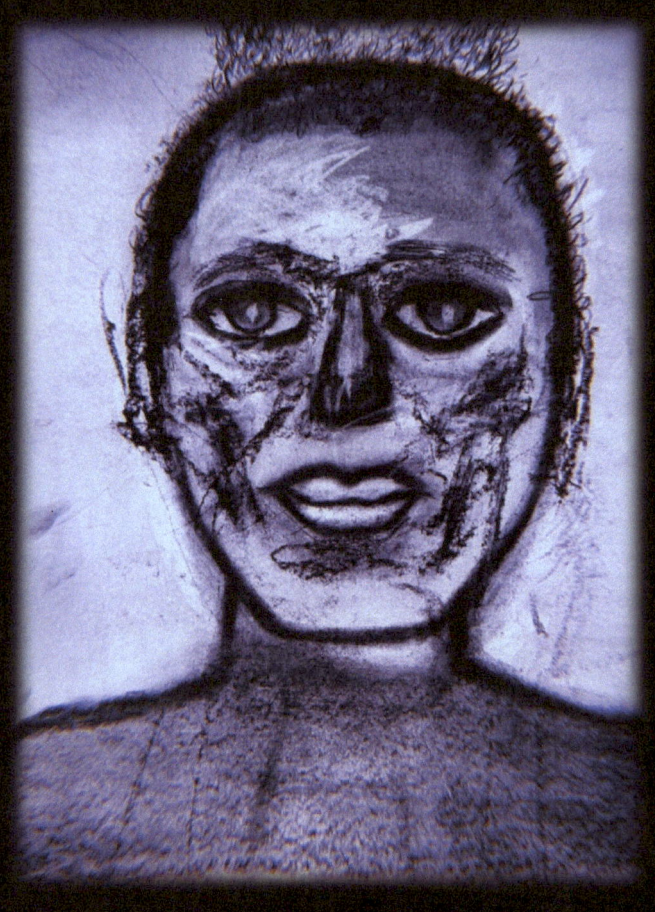

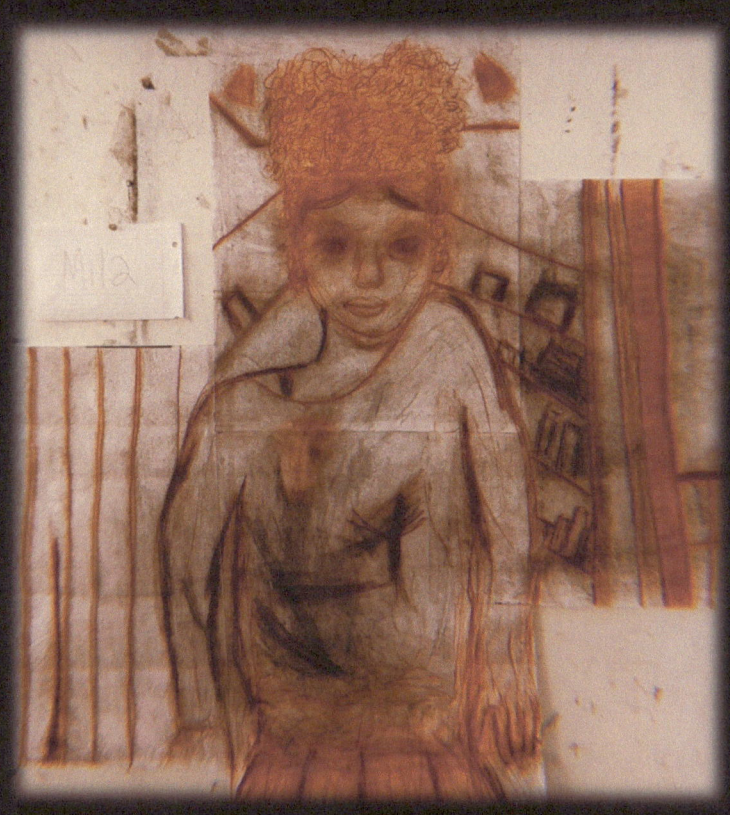

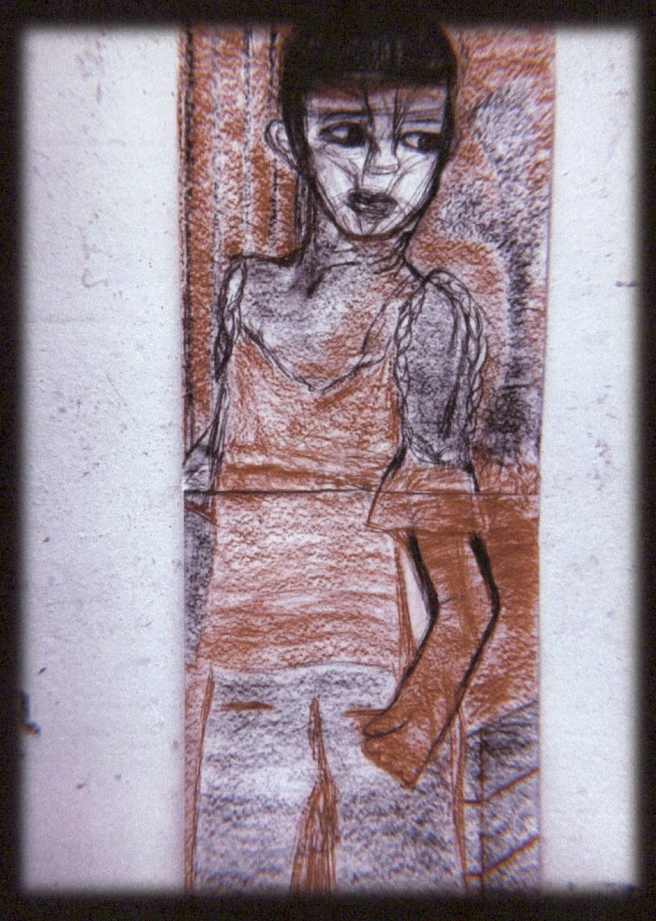

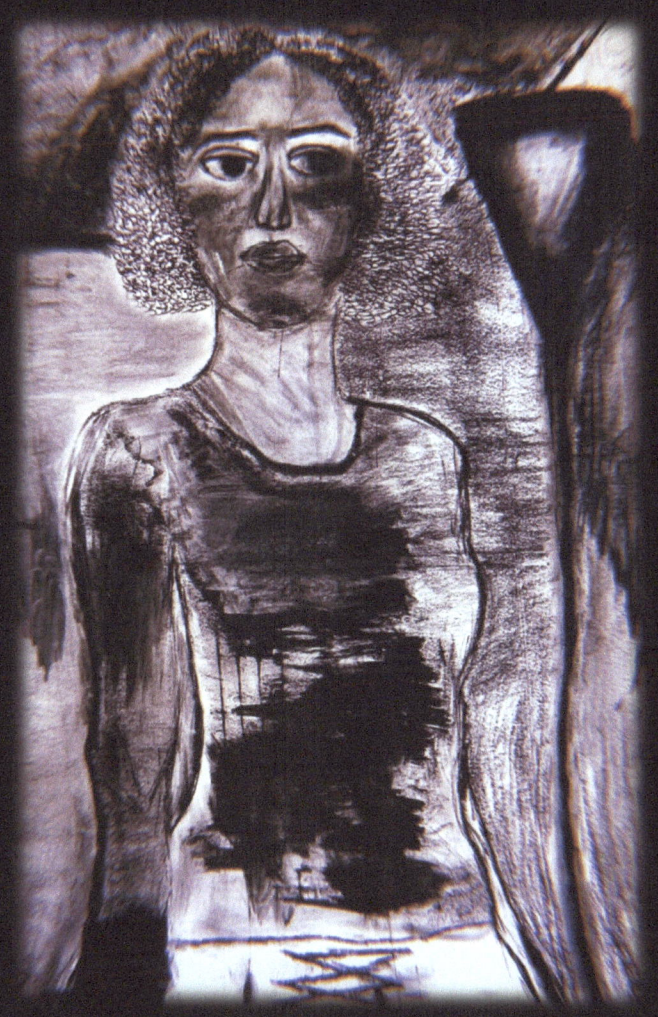

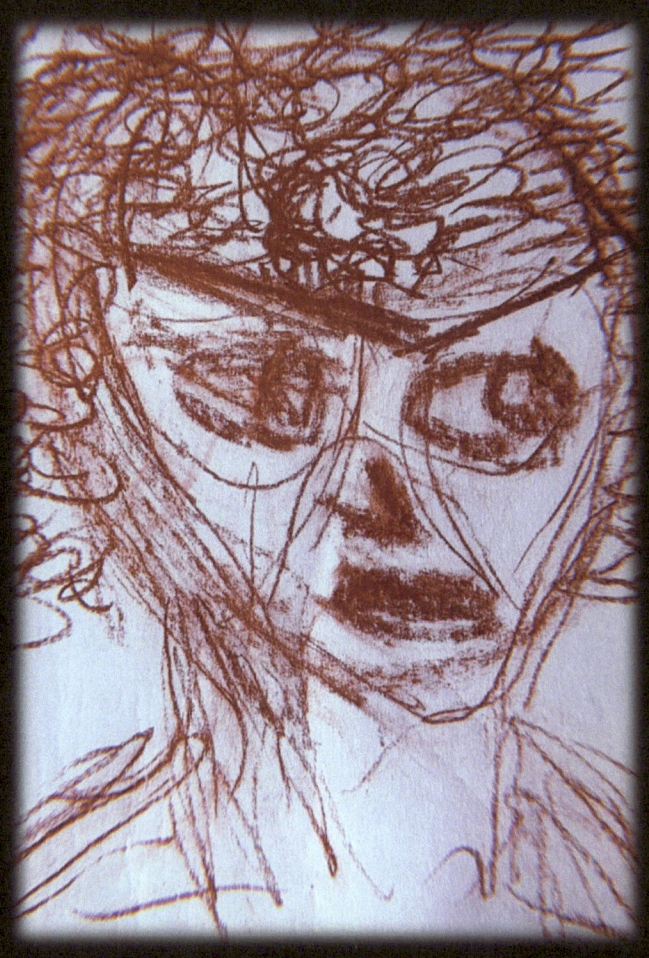

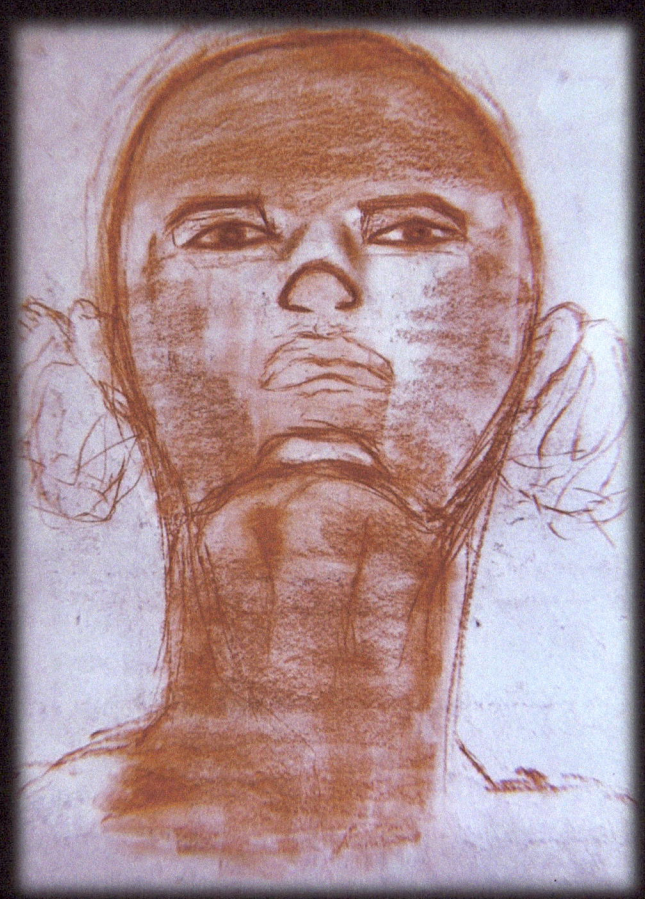

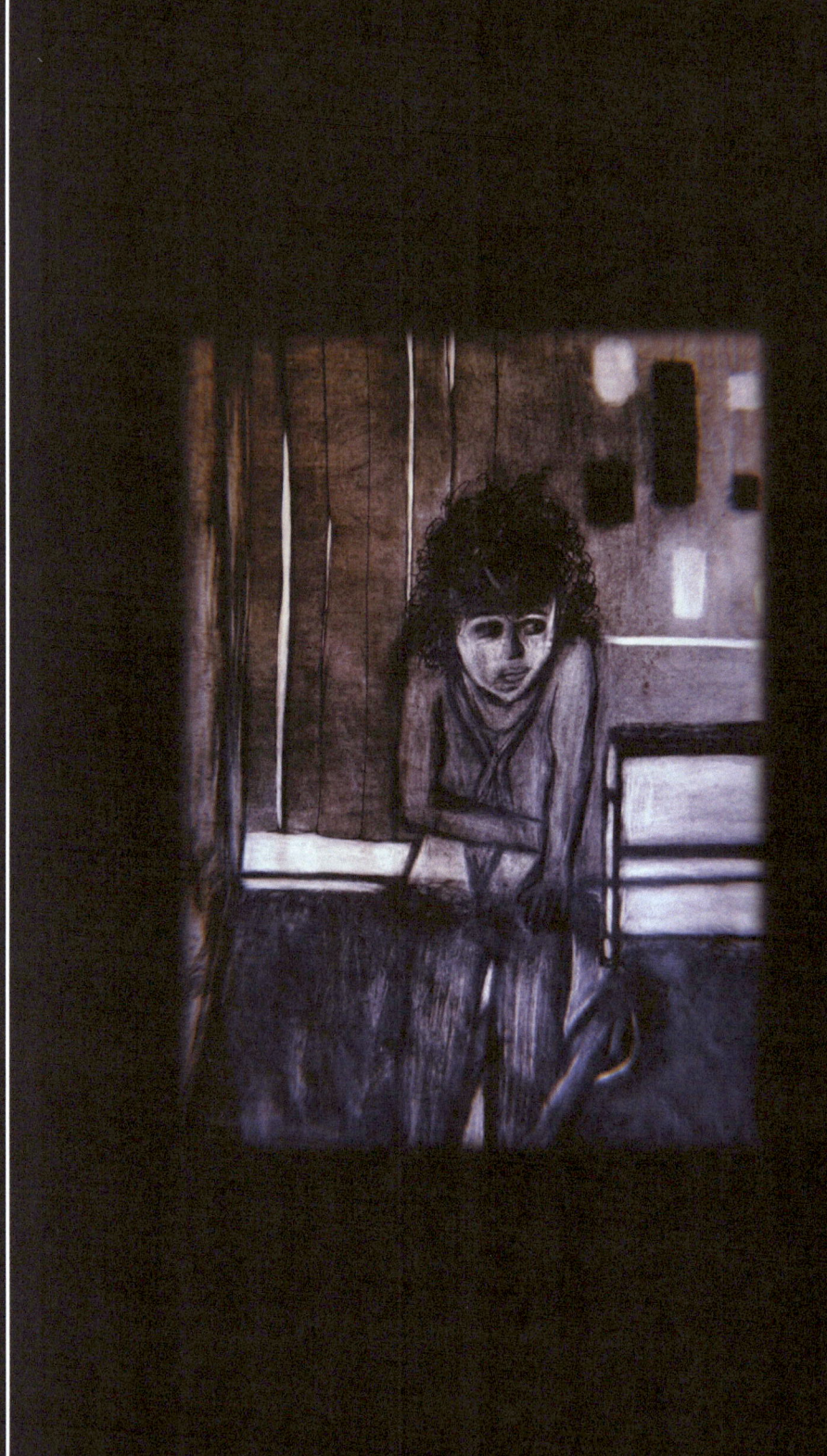

THANK

THE

YOU

END

About The Author

Mila Fox is an actress, singer, model, photographer, designer, and author. In addition to acting, running her fashion blog, CHIC-ipedia, and Mila Fox Photography, Mila is an advocate for Autism Awareness and Anti-Bullying.

www.ingramcontent.com/pod-product-compliance
Lightning Source LLC
Chambersburg PA
CBHW040920180526
45159CB00002BA/546